Harry Breidahl

This edition first published in 2002 in the United States of America by Chelsea House Publishers,
a subsidiary of Haights Cross Communications.

Chelsea House Publishers
1974 Sproul Road, Suite 400
Broomall, PA 19008-0914

The Chelsea House world wide web address is www.chelseahouse.com

Library of Congress Cataloging-in-Publication Data Applied for.
ISBN 0-7910-6618-5

First published in 2001 by
Macmillan Education Australia Pty Ltd
627 Chapel Street, South Yarra, Australia, 3141

Edited by Angelique Campbell-Muir
Text design by Cristina Neri
Cover design by Cristina Neri
Desktop publishing by Cristina Neri
Illustrations by Rhyll Plant
Printed in China

Acknowledgements
The author and the publishers are grateful to the following for permission to reproduce copyright material:

Cover photographs: Micro-organisms background, courtesy PhotoDisc; single dinoflagellate and coccolithophore, both courtesy Gustaaf M. Hallegraeff/University of Tasmania.

Auscape/Becca Saunders, p. 17; Auscape/John Cancalosi, p. 8 (left); Auscape/Tina Carvalho-Oxford Scientific Films, p. 9 (bottom left); Frank B. Llosa, pp. 3, 4 (left), 26–27 (bottom); Gustaaf M. Hallegraeff/University of Tasmania, pp. 1, 4 (right), 5 (top right and left), 10–16, 18, 19, 21, 24, 25 (both), 29 (right); Harry Breidahl, p. 22; Johnson Space Center/NASA, p. 27; © Kelvin Aitken, pp. 5 (bottom right), 28; National Oceanic and Atmospheric Administration/Department of Commerce/Neil Sullivan, University of Southern California, p. 9 (middle right); PhotoDisc, p. 9 (top left); Photolibrary.com/Dr. David Hall/SPL, pp. 5 (middle left), 20; Photolibrary.com/Philippe Plailly/SPL, pp. 6–7 (top), 23 (bottom); Photolibrary.com/Trevor Worden, p. 8 (right); Stephen Doggett/Department of Medical Entomology, Westmead Hospital, pp. 7 (bottom), 23 (top); The Picture Source/Terry Oakley, p. 29 (left).

While every care has been taken to trace and acknowledge copyright the publishers tender their apologies for any accidental infringement where copyright has proved untraceable. Where the attempt has been unsuccessful, the publishers welcome information that would redress the situation.

Contents

SEARCHING THE WORLD WIDE WEB

If you have access to the world wide web, you have a gateway to some fascinating information. You can also use the web to see photographs, watch short videos and even search for particular topics. In this book, useful search words appear like this— bioluminescence. Useful books and web sites are also listed on page 30.

Introducing phytoplankton

Plankton is the name given to minute **organisms** that drift about in water. The plant-like members of this drifting life are called **phytoplankton**. Although phytoplankton are like plants in some ways, they can be like animals in other ways. In this book we will concentrate on phytoplankton that live in the sea.

Despite being incredibly small, phytoplankton are among the most beautiful organisms on Earth. They come in many fascinating shapes and forms. Some are round, like little pillboxes. Others are long and thin. Whip-like attachments are common, as are spikes, spines and shields. Some phytoplankton live alone. Others form long chains.

HOW DO YOU SAY IT?

plankton: **plank**-ton
phytoplankton: fite-o-**plank**-ton

Although they are too small to see without a microscope, lots of phytoplankton together can change the color of water (see pages 26–27).

The most common phytoplankton in the sea are called diatoms. They are **single-celled** organisms with glass skeletons. Many of these skeletons have beautiful shapes (see pages 12–13).

Dinoflagellates have two whip-like attachments. Although they can make their own food, some dinoflagellates feed on other organisms. Some even live inside other organisms (see pages 14–17).

HOW DO YOU SAY IT?

diatoms: die-**a**-toms
dinoflagellates: dine-o-**fla**-jell-ates

Coccolithophores are just as beautiful as diatoms. Coccolithophores are covered with ornate shield-shaped plates. They and their plates are very important in the history of the Earth (see pages 18–19).

Some phytoplankton, such as the plant-like bacteria known as cyanobacteria, can affect human health (see page 20).

Phytoplankton are the main food producers in the ocean. Without phytoplankton whales and almost all other animals in the ocean would not exist (see pages 28–29).

HOW DO YOU SAY IT?

coccolithophores: cock-o-**lith**-o-fors
cyanobacteria: sigh-an-o-back-**tear**-re-a

Background

Measuring phytoplankton

To get an idea of just how small phytoplankton are, you need to think about scale and measurement. The measurement units used in this book belong to the **metric system**. In the metric system, the smallest commonly used unit is a millimeter (mm). (If you are used to feet and inches, 100 millimeters equals about 4 inches.) A human eye can see objects as small as one-tenth of a millimeter across—any smaller than that and you would need a magnifying glass or a microscope to see clearly.

Because phytoplankton are so small, you also need to be familiar with the units of measurement used for anything smaller than a millimeter. This is where the metric system is easy to follow because each new unit is smaller by a factor of 10, 100 or 1000. Counting down in lots of 1000, there are three basic metric units of measurement that you need to remember:

- one millimeter (mm) is $^{1}/_{1000}$ of a meter
- one micrometer (μm) is $^{1}/_{1000}$ of a millimeter
- one nanometer (nm) is $^{1}/_{1000}$ of a micrometer.

Phytoplankton are usually between 5 and 100 micrometers in size.

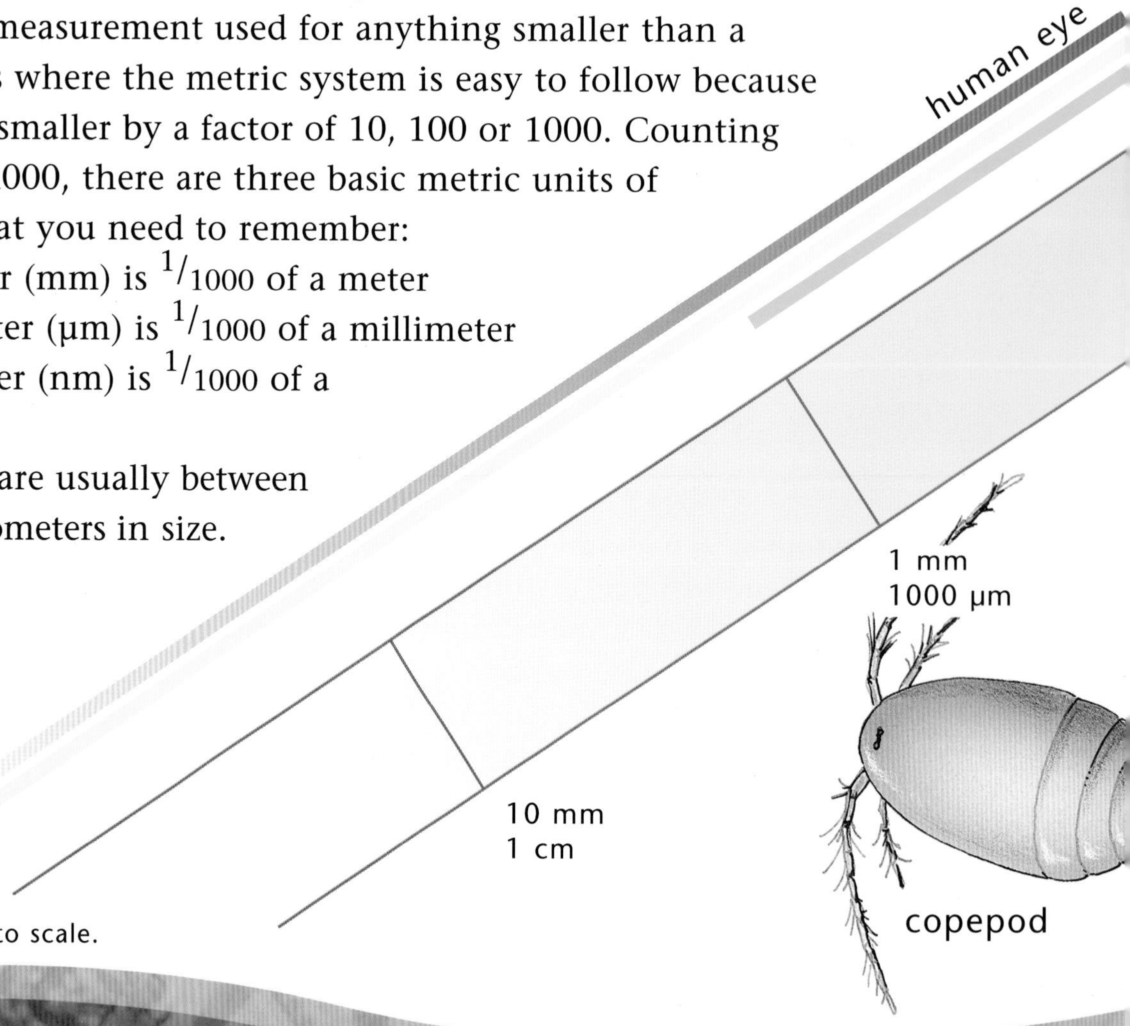

human eye

10 mm
1 cm

1 mm
1000 μm

copepod

Illustrations not drawn to scale.

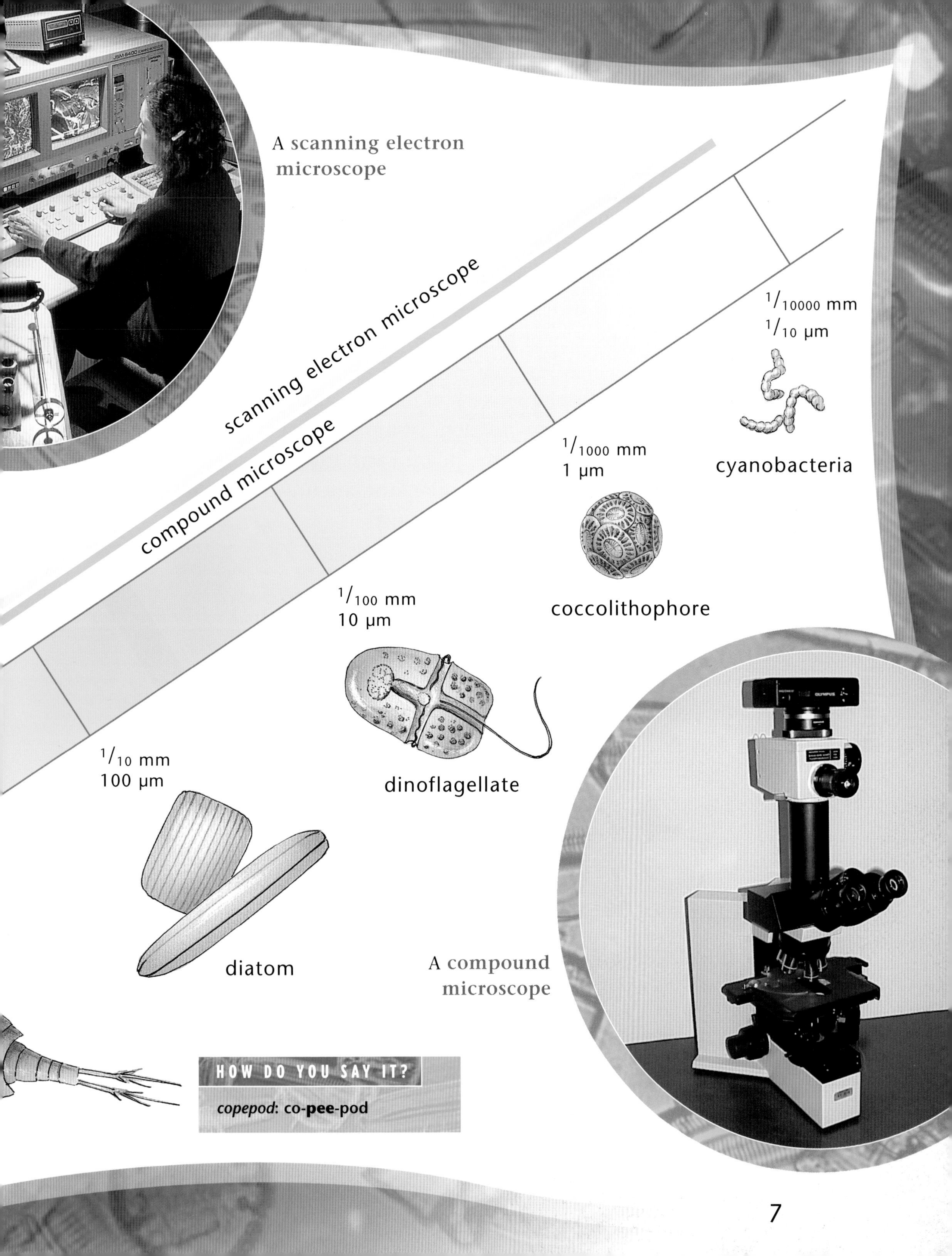

HOW DO YOU SAY IT?

copepod: co-**pee**-pod

Sorting life on Earth into kingdoms

Until quite recently biologists divided life on Earth into two broad groups—the plant kingdom and the animal kingdom. The main difference between these two groups is that plants stay in one place and usually make their own food, while animals move about and feed on other organisms. Under this system, phytoplankton were called plants.

Since the discovery of microscopic organisms, this simple two-kingdom system no longer works. One new system sorts life on Earth into five kingdoms. Almost all phytoplankton are now placed in the Kingdom Protoctista.

Kingdom Animalia

Animals are organisms that eat other organisms. Animals are all **multi-celled**. In the ocean, small animals called zooplankton eat the smaller phytoplankton. Larger animals, including whales, eat zooplankton.

Kingdom Plantae

Plants are organisms that use sunlight to make their own food. Plants are all multi-celled. Trees, grasses, ferns and mosses belong to the plant kingdom. Seaweeds and phytoplankton used to be part of the plant kingdom, but are now part of the Kingdom Protoctista.

Kingdom Fungi

Fungi, such as mushrooms and toadstools, were once thought to be plants. Now they are placed in a kingdom of their own. Fungi get their energy by decomposing (breaking down) other organisms.

Kingdom Protoctista

Most members of this group, like phytoplankton, are microscopic. Most are single-celled. A few, such as seaweeds, are multi-celled. Some members of this group eat other organisms. Others make their own food. Some can do both.

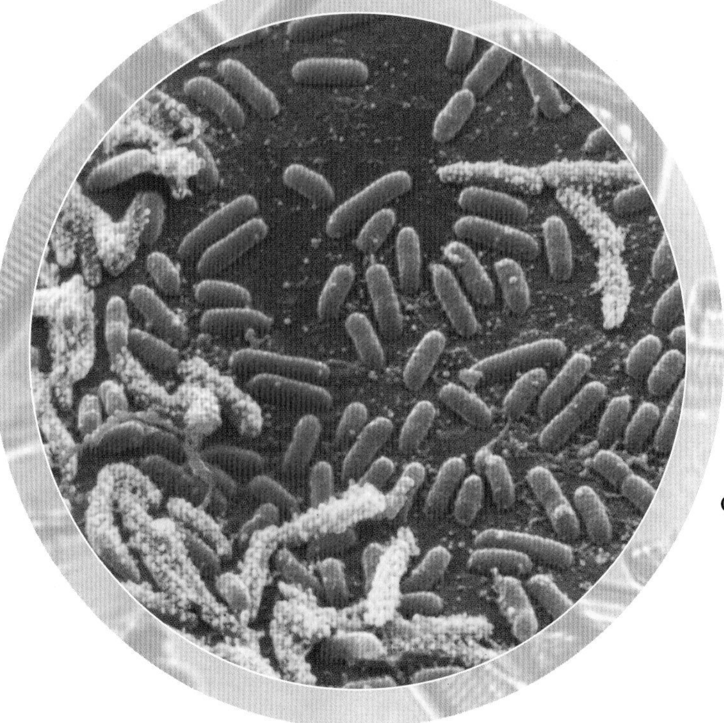

Kingdom Monera

The members of the Kingdom Monera are all microscopic organisms called **microbes** Another name for them is bacteria. They are all single-celled. One type of bacteria, called cyanobacteria, uses sunlight to make its own food. Other bacteria feed by breaking down organic (living) material.

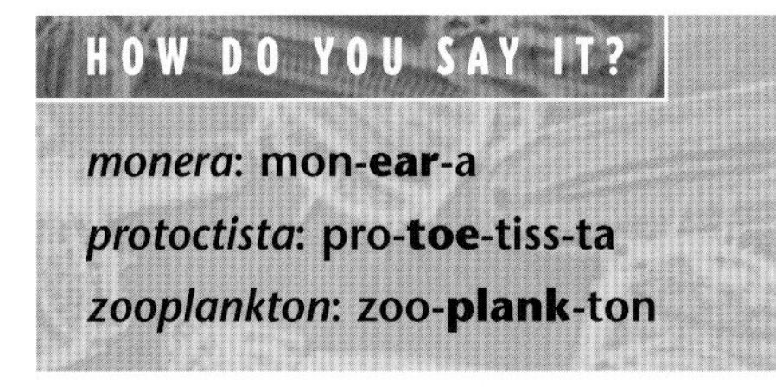

HOW DO YOU SAY IT?

monera: mon-**ear**-a
protoctista: pro-**toe**-tiss-ta
zooplankton: zoo-**plank**-ton

The life of a drifter

The old two-kingdom system works well on land where plants are rooted in one place and animals move about. However, phytoplankton live in water and do not easily fit into this system. Although they have the plant-like ability to make their own food, they are also free to drift through the water and some can even swim. Some phytoplankton also eat other organisms. This is why biologists now classify phytoplankton and plants in separate kingdoms.

Because phytoplankton use sunlight to make food, they need to stay near the surface of the water. In the ocean, the deeper you go the darker it gets. To get the sunlight they need, phytoplankton must stay within 30 meters (100 feet) of the surface. To do this, some phytoplankton, such as dinoflagellates, use whip-like attachments, called flagella, to swim about. However, dinoflagellates cannot swim very well. Other phytoplankton, such as diatoms, stay near the surface by storing oil inside their bodies. This oil is lighter than sea water and so it helps them to float.

Dinoflagellates are phytoplankton that can swim about weakly. They do so using two whip-like attachments, called flagella. Although dinoflagellates can swim, they are not strong swimmers and are still regarded as drifters.

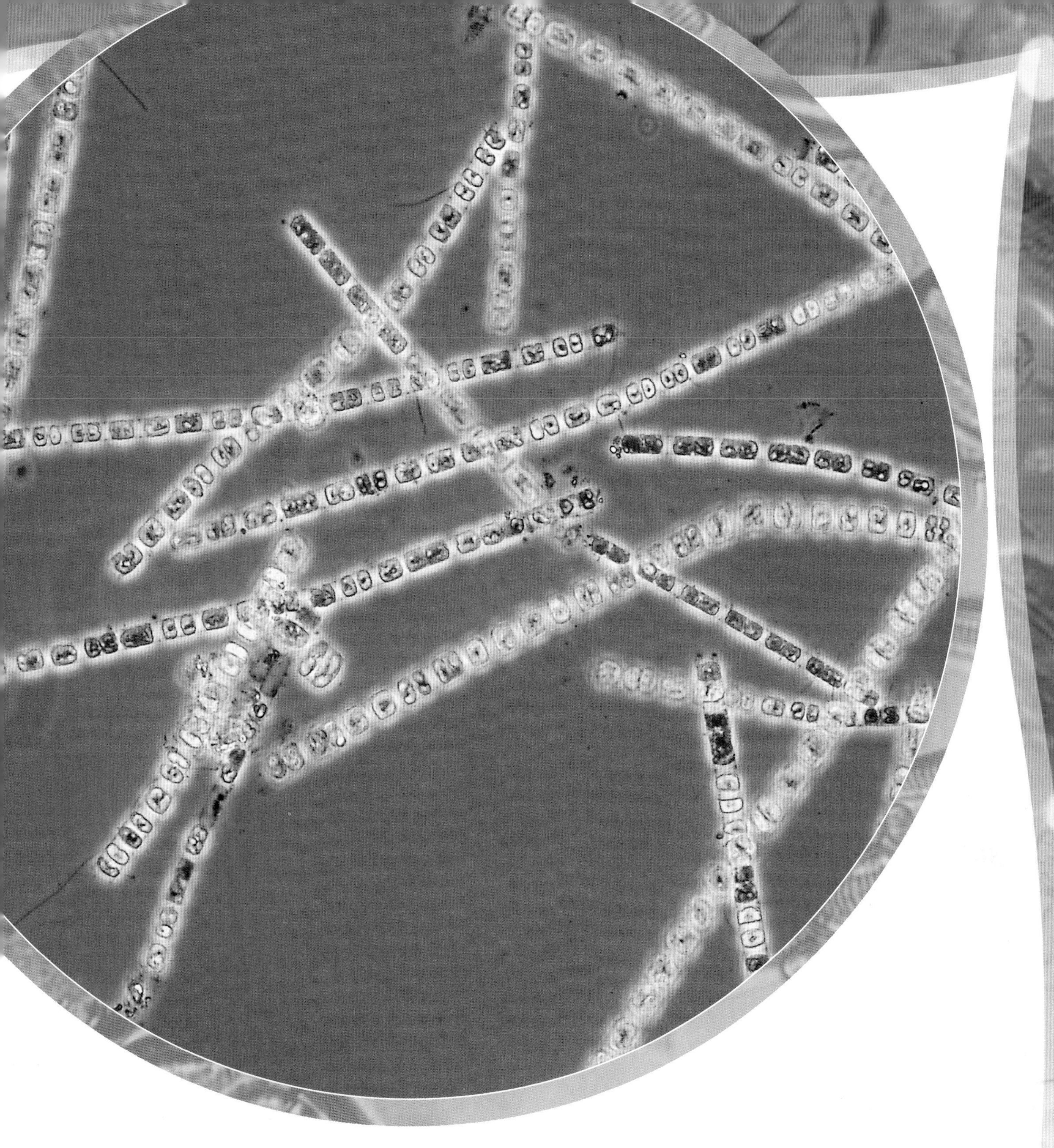

HOW DO YOU SAY IT?

flagella: fla-**jell**-a

As well as using oil to float near the surface, some diatoms have long glass spines that act like parachutes to keep them near the surface. Other diatoms link together in long chains, as shown here. Although diatoms do not have flagella, some can glide about on a carpet of slime.

Phytoplankton

Diatoms—living in glass houses

Diatoms are the most common kind of phytoplankton. Each individual diatom is a single **cell** inside two glass shells. These two glass shells are shaped so that one fits over the other like the lid on a container. The glass shells are full of small holes that let materials pass in and out. These holes are arranged in intricate lines and patterns. Even though diatoms are single-celled, some kinds link together to form chains.

There are two main types of diatoms: those shaped like a cylinder, and those that are long and thin like a pencil. The pencil-shaped diatoms can glide around in the water. Cylindrical diatoms cannot move. Diatoms can reproduce very quickly. In the right conditions, a single diatom can produce a billion offspring in just one month. This sort of rapid growth in numbers is called a bloom.

Although they are incredibly small, diatoms, such as this stunning fan-shaped colony, are among the most beautiful organisms on Earth. We can use a compound microscope to see diatoms more clearly. A compound microscope shines light through an object. This shows that diatoms are actually golden-brown in color.

A scanning electron microscope can show tiny details such as the fine holes in a diatom's glass shells. When diatoms die, the glass shells build up on the sea floor. Vast collections of these shells form a rock called diatomaceous earth. Diatomaceous earth can be used to make many different things. It was once used in toothpaste!

Dinoflagellates—whirling whips

Dinoflagellates are a type of phytoplankton that can usually move about. A dinoflagellate has two whip-like attachments called flagella. One is stretched-out like a tail, and the other is wrapped around its middle. To move about, a dinoflagellate wriggles its flagella. When both flagella move together, the dinoflagellate spins or whirls forward. (The name dinoflagellate means 'whirling whip'.) Although most dinoflagellates use sunlight to make their own food, like plants, some feed on other organisms, like animals.

Dinoflagellates are found in both fresh water and sea water. Most dinoflagellates drift around in the sea with other types of plankton, but may also be found living in sand. Some even live inside other organisms (see pages 16–17). Like diatoms, dinoflagellates can reproduce rapidly in the right conditions. Dinoflagellates are a red-brown color, and massive blooms of them can make the sea look red. Blooms of dinoflagellates are called **red tides**. Some red tides may be caused by toxic dinoflagellates (dinoflagellates that produce poisons). These poisons can kill marine life and humans that eat affected seafood. Dinoflagellates can also affect the color of the sea in other ways (see pages 26–27).

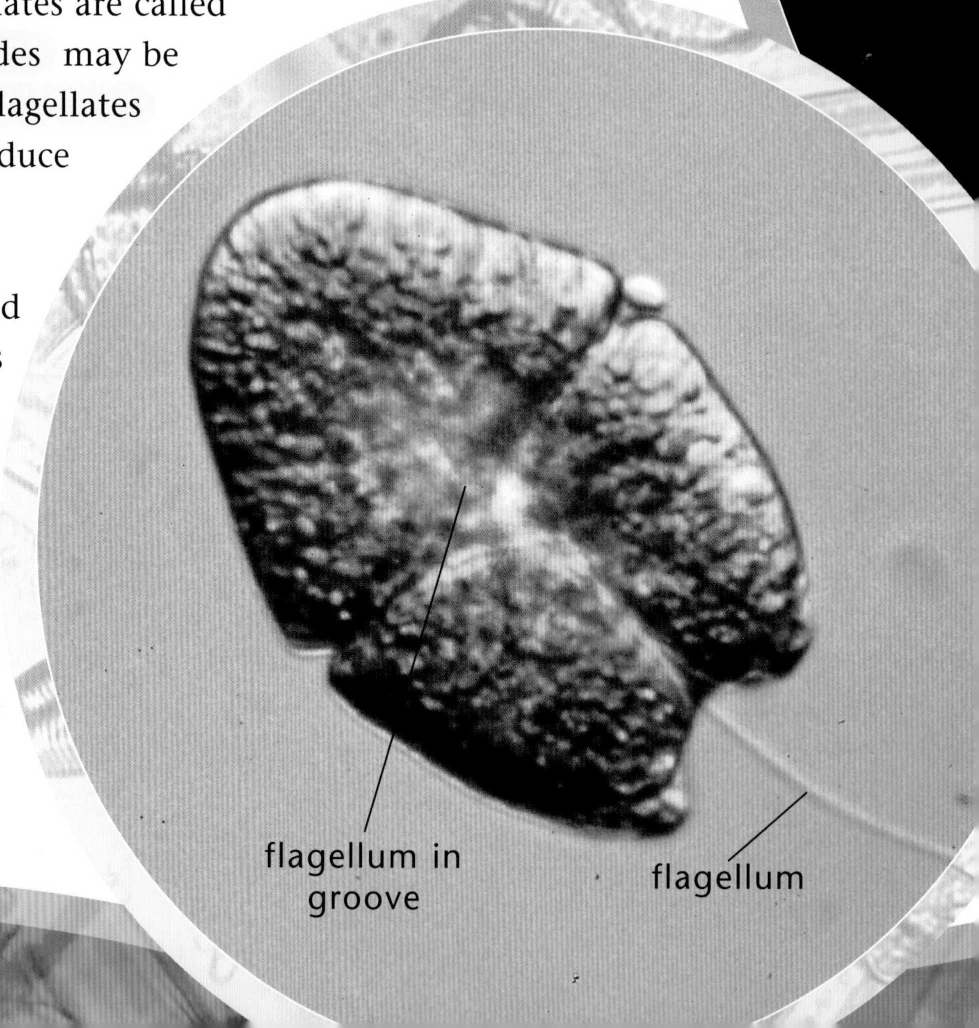

flagellum

flagellum

Scanning electron microscopes show much more detail, such as the central groove that holds one of the two flagella. They also show the plates that protect a dinoflagellate's body. These plates are made of a material called **cellulose**, which is the same material plants use to make wood.

Many dinoflagellates are large enough to see using a compound microscope. These microscopes often give a good idea of the red-brown color of dinoflagellates, but do not show other details.

Zooxanthellae—living inside corals

Not all phytoplankton drift about in the ocean—there are some that stay in the one place. The best examples of 'stay-at-home' phytoplankton are called zooxanthellae. Zooxanthellae are dinoflagellates that live inside animals such as corals. Reef-building corals are marine animals that live in massive colonies and build a hard skeleton made of limestone. Each individual coral animal is called a polyp, and it is within the flesh of each polyp that the zooxanthellae live.

This close partnership between two different organisms works well. The zooxanthellae use sunlight to make their own food and produce **oxygen**. They share the food and oxygen with the polyp, and receive both shelter and nutrients from the polyp in return. In this way, phytoplankton contribute directly to coral reefs. Corals are the main organisms responsible for building reefs, but they cannot do this without zooxanthellae.

HOW DO YOU SAY IT?

zooxanthellae: zoo-zan-**thell**-ee

Zooxanthellae are tiny and can only be seen using a compound microscope. They live in corals in shallow tropical water. These warm waters are so clear that there is plenty of sunlight for the zooxanthellae. The clear waters lack nutrients, though, so very few other phytoplankton can live here.

Zooxanthellae are very colorful organisms. Because there are millions of tiny zooxanthellae in each polyp, they contribute to the vivid colors of the reef-building corals in which they live. More importantly, the food that zooxanthellae produce helps coral polyps to build massive structures, such as the Great Barrier Reef.

Coccolithophores—dazzling discs

Coccolithophores are very small but incredibly spectacular. Each single-celled coccolithophore gets its weird and wonderful appearance from the minute, shield-shaped plates that surround its cell. These plates are called coccoliths. Coccoliths are only 1 to 3 micrometers across. This means that over 1,000 coccoliths would fit on the period at the end of this sentence. Unlike other phytoplankton, coccolithophores use a material called calcite to build their plates.

When a coccolithophore dies, its coccoliths fall off and settle at the bottom of the sea. In this way, coccolithophores dump lots of calcite on the sea floor each year. They have been doing this for many millions of years, which has produced large amounts of a rock called chalk. Coccolithophores have at least two separate stages in their life cycle. During one stage of their life cycle they are covered in coccoliths. This is when they look their most beautiful. During the second stage, they have no coccoliths, and have two flagella instead. Scientists once thought these two stages were actually different organisms.

HOW DO YOU SAY IT?

coccoliths: cock-o-**liths**

Coccoliths are so small that they can only be seen clearly using a scanning electron microscope. It is hard to believe that something so intricate could be produced by a living thing, especially one so small. The distinctive shapes of coccoliths allow biologists to identify different coccolithophores.

One of the best known coccolithophores is called *Emiliania huxleyi*. This widespread coccolithophore is named after the famous English scientist Thomas Huxley. Huxley was one of the first to find coccoliths in sediment from the sea floor. He was also the first person to use the word 'coccolith'. Massive blooms of *Emiliania huxleyi* can turn the ocean almost white (see page 26).

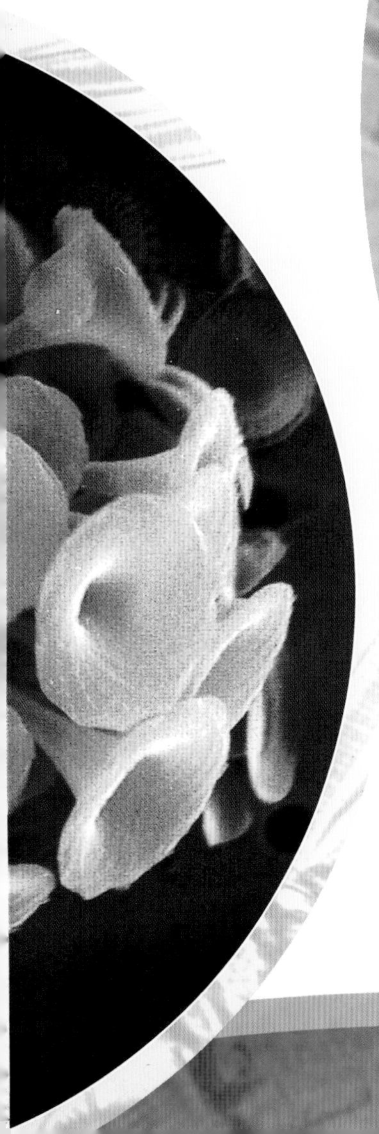

Other diminutive drifters

Hauling a plankton net through the sea is a bit like taking a lucky dip—you never know what surprises you will turn up. Although diatoms and dinoflagellates are the most common kinds of phytoplankton, there are other microscopic organisms that spend all or part of their lives drifting about the sea. This means that the variety of diminutive drifters captured by your net may be quite great. At times, you may collect less common organisms, such as silicoflagellates.

The organisms discussed so far belong to the Kingdom Protoctista. However, there are other plant-like plankton that belong to a second kingdom, the Kingdom Monera (organisms with very small and simply constructed cells). They are the plant-like bacteria called cyanobacteria. Cyanobacteria are regarded as being phytoplankton because they use sunlight to make their own food and because they drift about in water. Like other phytoplankton, cyanobacteria are single-celled organisms. Sometimes they join together to form long chains.

HOW DO YOU SAY IT?

silicoflagellates: sil-ik-o-**fla**-jell-ates

Because their cells are so much smaller than other phytoplankton, cyanobacteria are easy to recognize. They are also a distinctive dark blue-green color (the color in this photograph has been added artificially). Large blooms of cyanobacteria sometimes occur in freshwater. Blooms of cyanobacteria turn the water a dark green color. These blooms can be poisonous to humans and other animals.

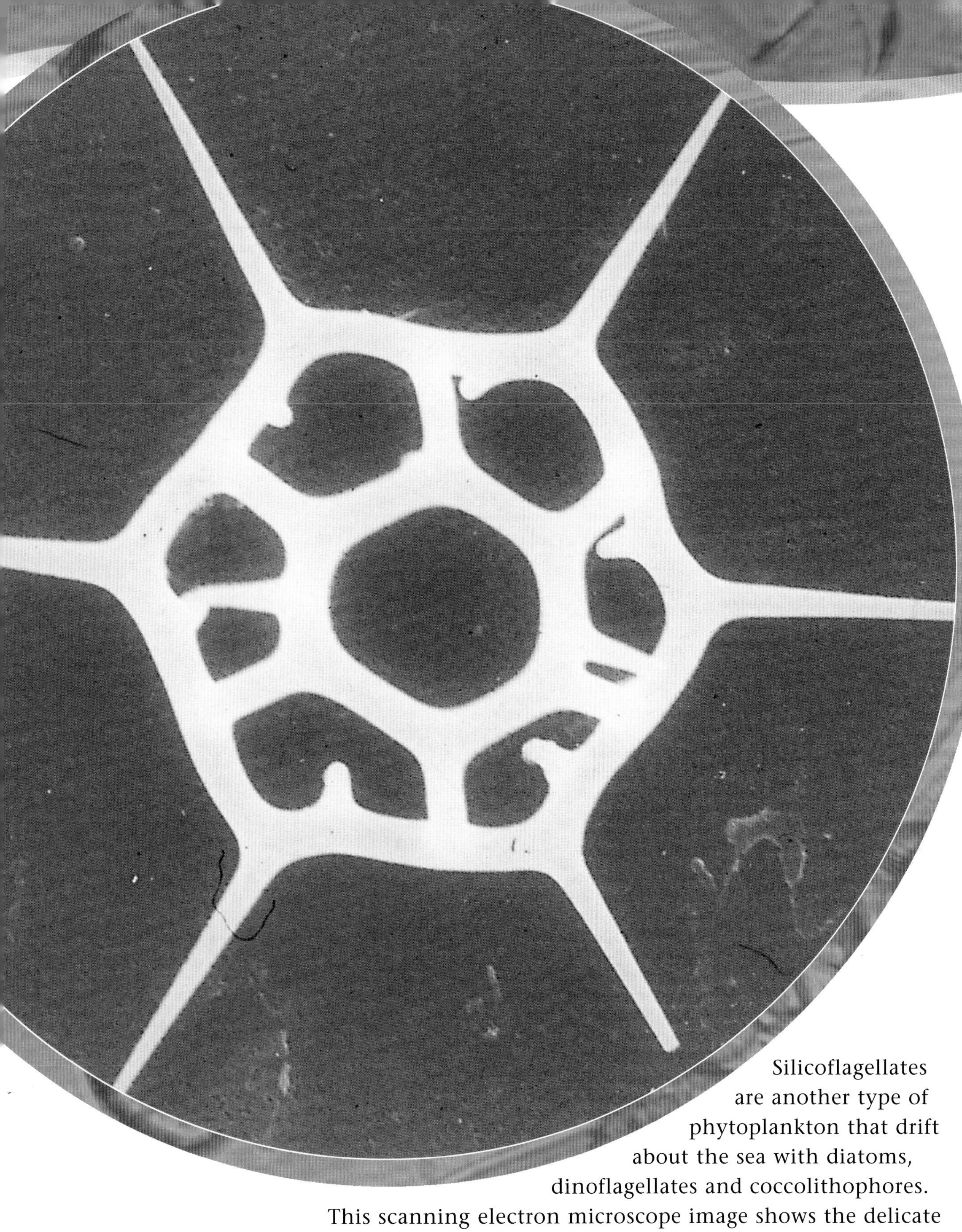

Silicoflagellates are another type of phytoplankton that drift about the sea with diatoms, dinoflagellates and coccolithophores. This scanning electron microscope image shows the delicate glass shell of a dead silicoflagellate.

Technology
Nets and microscopes

Phytoplankton is collected with a fine-mesh net, called a plankton net. You can make your own plankton net by sewing old pantyhose onto a wire frame (such as an old coat hanger). Commercially made plankton nets are also available through scientific suppliers. To collect the plankton, simply drag your net through the water. This is usually done by towing the net behind a boat, but you can also do it as you walk along a pier.

Because phytoplankton are so small, you will need a microscope to see them. There are two main kinds of microscopes: compound microscopes, like those found in school laboratories, and high-tech devices known as electron microscopes. They both have a lens or a series of **lenses** that make small things look bigger.

Commercially made plankton nets, like the one shown here, are the best way to collect plankton. Because phytoplankton are incredibly small, usually between 5 and 100 micrometers across, the mesh used to make this net must be very fine. The jar at the end is used to hold the phytoplankton.

A compound microscope uses two or more lenses to magnify the image of an object. A compound microscope requires light to be shone through an object. This means that the object must first be placed on a glass slide, a process that results in flat, two-dimensional images.

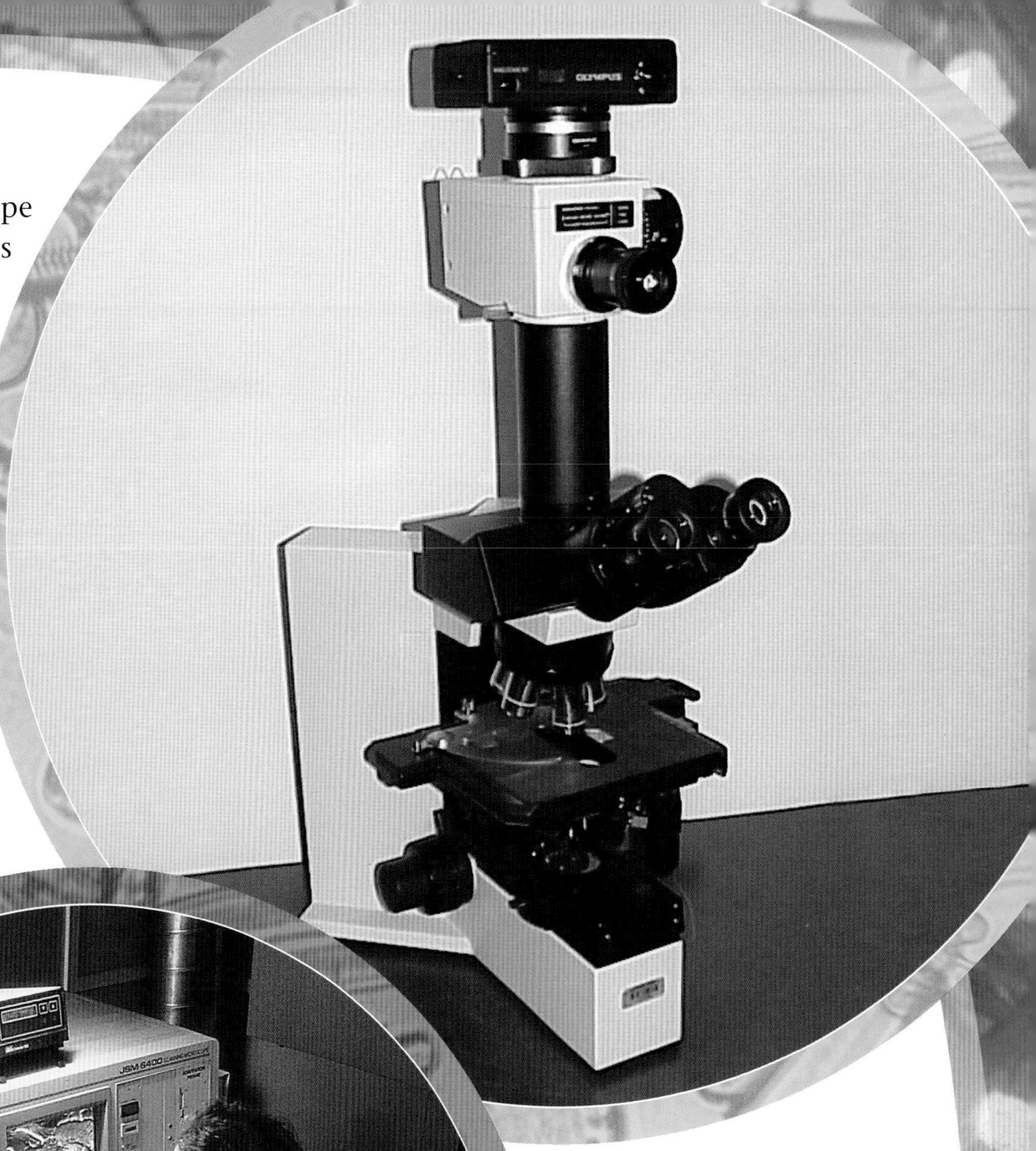

A second kind of microscope, called a scanning electron microscope (sem), uses a beam of electrons instead of light. They are very expensive microscopes but produce very detailed three-dimensional images. Because electrons cannot show color, sem pictures are usually shown in black and white.

Profile of a marine biologist

Professor Gustaaf Hallegraeff

Gustaaf Hallegraeff grew up in the Netherlands. When he was six years old, an uncle gave him a little microscope. Gustaaf used his microscope to explore the microscopic world, including phytoplankton, that lived in rainwater tanks. After graduating from college, Professor Hallegraeff studied the phytoplankton found in polluted Dutch lakes. He later accepted a job at the Commonwealth Scientific and Industrial Research Organisation (CSIRO) marine laboratories in Australia.

In Australia, Professor Hallegraeff specializes in the study of marine phytoplankton. When he moved to the CSIRO marine laboratories in Hobart, in 1984, Professor Hallegraeff discovered vast numbers of a dinoflagellate called *Gymnodinium catenatum* in the Derwent River. The Derwent River is a major Australian port. *Gymnodinium catenatum* is one of the dinoflagellates that causes red tides. These toxic dinoflagellates release poisons that kill marine life, and humans who eat affected seafood. Professor Hallegraeff was able to show that *Gymnodinium catenatum* was most likely transported to the Derwent River aboard ships from Japan.

Professor Hallegraeff achieved his dream of working on the ocean and in the sun when he moved from the Netherlands to Australia. Although he spends some time working on boats, he also does a lot of work in laboratories.

Gustaaf Hallegraeff is currently Associate Professor and Head of the School of Plant Science at the University of Tasmania, in Hobart. He specializes in the study of phytoplankton. These organisms are so small that microscopes are an important tool in Professor Hallegraeff's work.

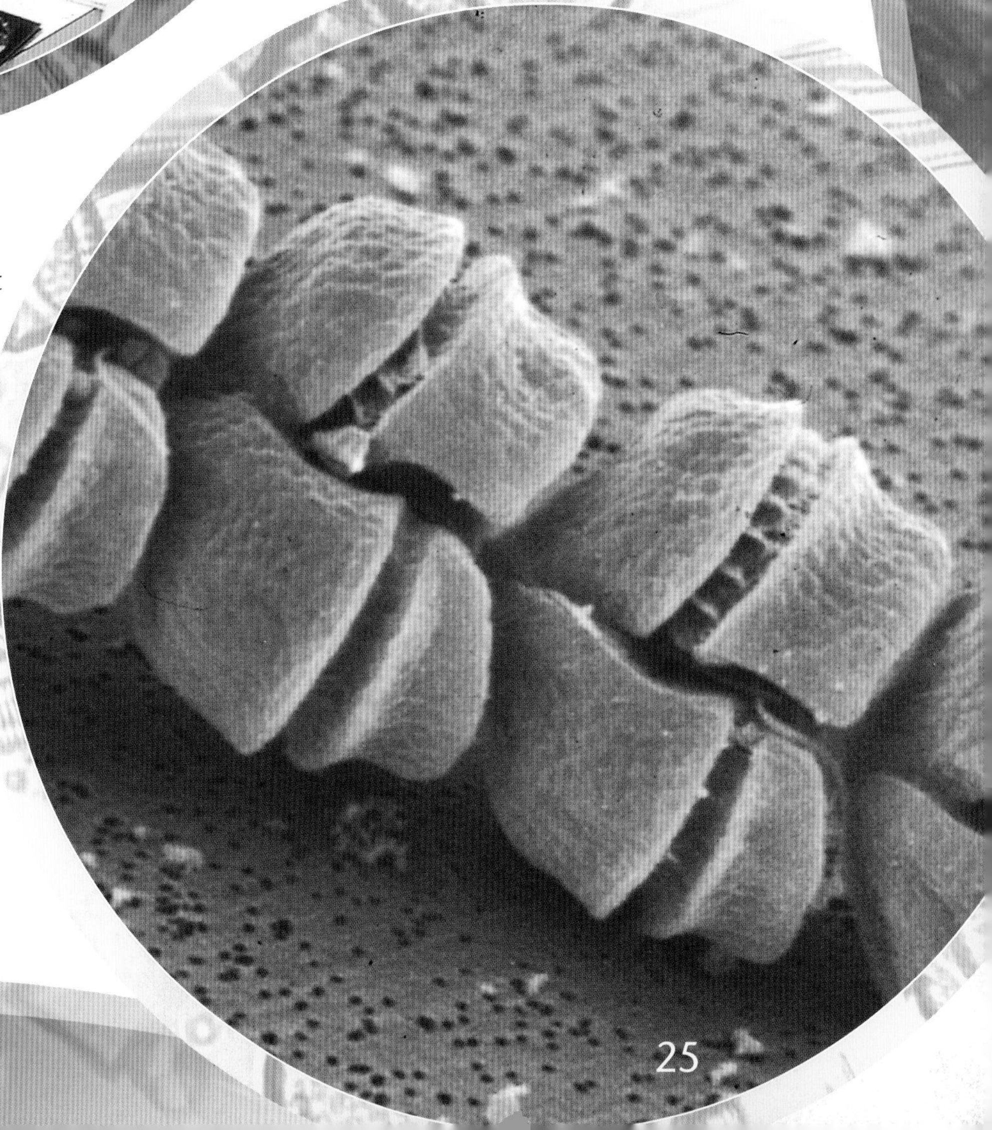

Professor Hallegraeff's first plankton haul in the Derwent River turned up vast numbers of the toxic dinoflagellate *Gymnodinium catenatum*. Since then, he has taken a leading role in the study of these deadly organisms.

What phytoplankton means to you

Blooms and bioluminescence

The basic color of sea water is blue. This is easy to see in clear ocean waters. However, in shallow water closer to shore the sea often has a blue-green color. One thing that can cause this blue-green color in sea water is phytoplankton. At certain times billions of phytoplankton can fill the water. This is called a bloom. Blooms can change the color of the sea to bright green, red (red tides) or even milky-white.

The ability of living things to produce light is known as bioluminescence. Many organisms, including dinoflagellates, are capable of bioluminescence. They do so by mixing two chemicals that glow when combined. Bioluminescence in the sea can be enchanting, especially when there are vast numbers of dinoflagellates in the water. Any movement, such as a wave breaking, someone swimming, or a boat moving through the water, sets off the eerie cold-blue glow.

HOW DO YOU SAY IT?

bioluminescence: buy-o-loom-in-**es**-sence

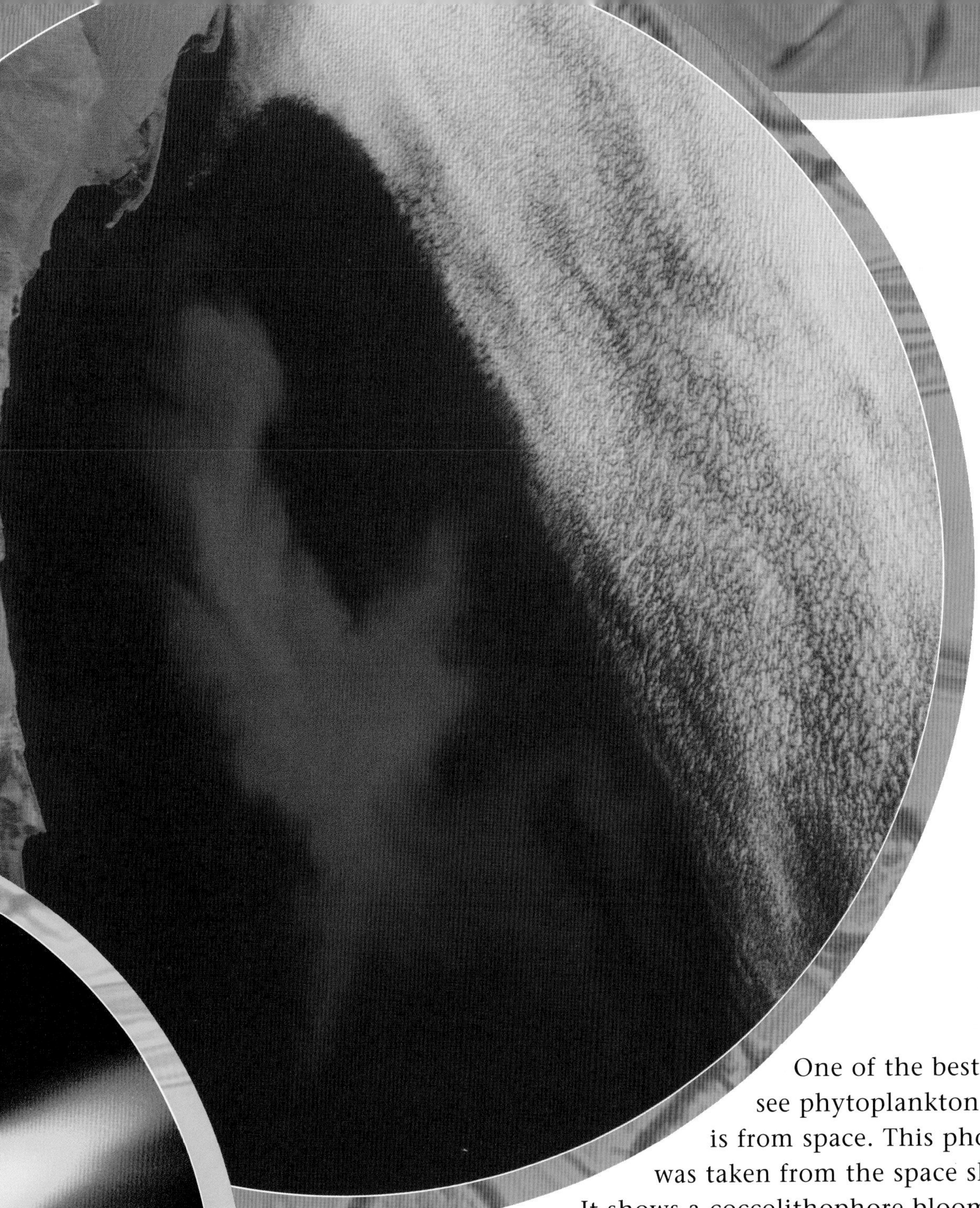

One of the best ways to see phytoplankton blooms is from space. This photograph was taken from the space shuttle. It shows a coccolithophore bloom that turned the waters of the Atlantic Ocean milky-white in color.

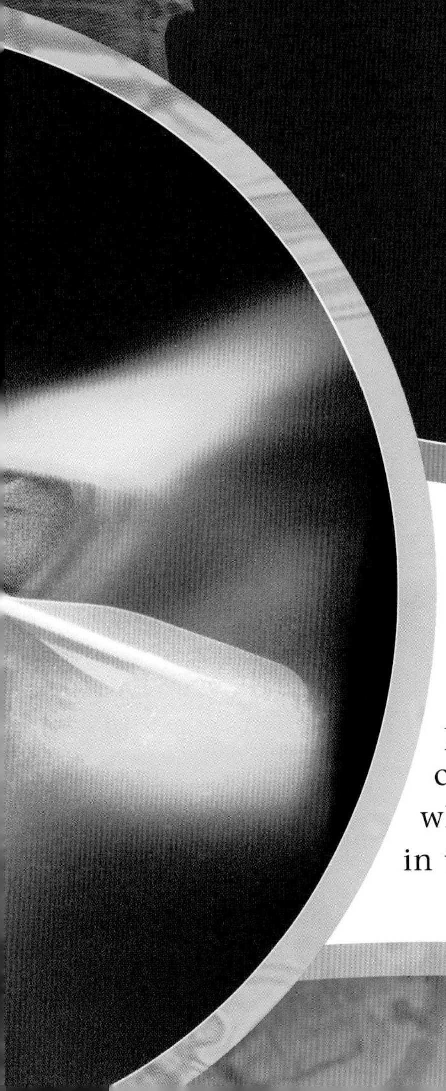

Mosquito Bay, on the island of Vieques in Puerto Rico, is probably the best place in the world to see bioluminescence created by dinoflagellates. Unlike other parts of the world, where bioluminescence is an occasional event, dinoflagellates in this bay glow every night.

Have you thanked phytoplankton today?

Without phytoplankton the Earth would be a very different place:

- the temperature would be much hotter
- there would be much less oxygen for us to breathe
- there would be very little life in the oceans
- we would not have gasoline to drive about in cars.

Phytoplankton help make all of this possible with photosynthesis. Photosynthesis is the process by which phytoplankton and plants use sunlight to make their own food.

During photosynthesis, plants and phytoplankton use sunlight to combine carbon dioxide (a gas) and water to produce sugars (food) and oxygen. This means that phytoplankton:

- help to keep the Earth cool by using up carbon dioxide
- produce about half of the Earth's oxygen
- start the food chains that almost all larger marine animals rely on
- created the gasoline we use to power cars.

When people talk of conservation they are usually referring to big animals, such as whales. However, phytoplankton are equally important. In fact, without plankton to feed on, whales and almost all other animals in the sea would not exist.

When the phytoplankton that lived in the ocean millions of years ago died, their bodies fell to the sea floor and were buried by sediments. Organic chemicals from these buried bodies collect underground to make crude oil. We use crude oil to make the gasoline that fuels cars.

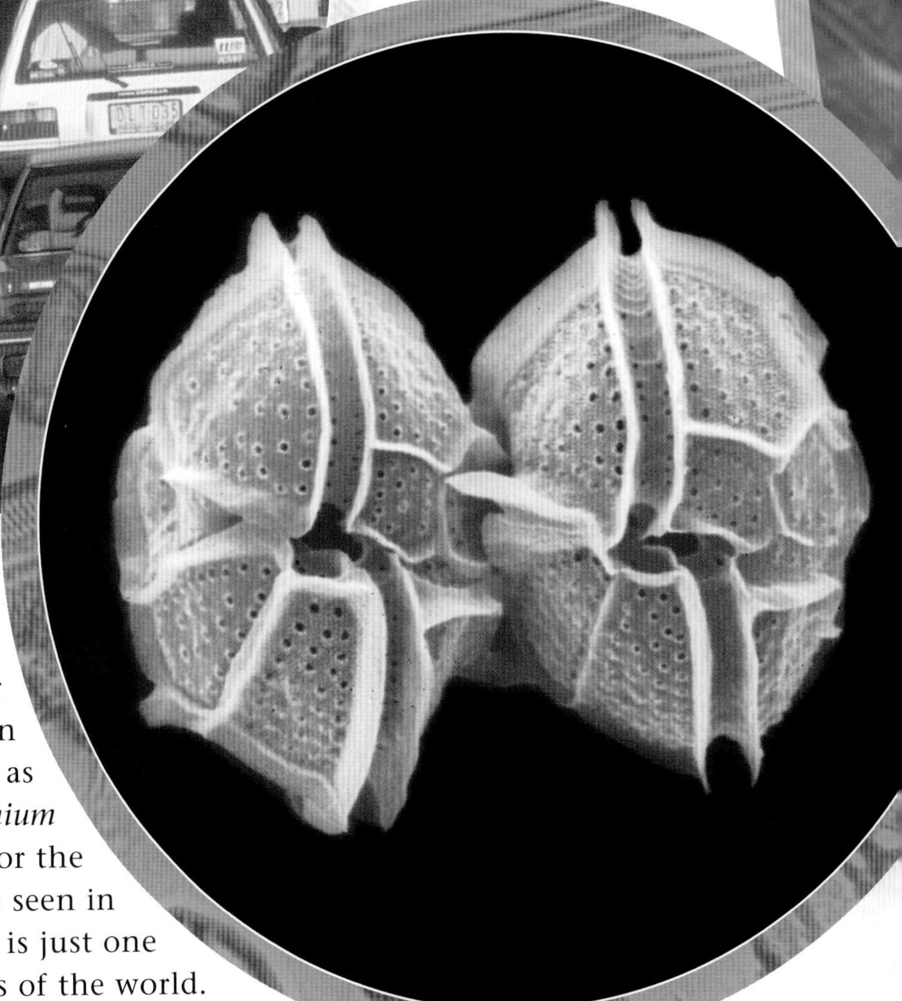

Phytoplankton make up for being small by being present in incredible numbers. Some, such as the dinoflagellate *Pyrodinium bahamenese*, are responsible for the spectacular bioluminescence seen in Mosquito Bay (see page 27). This is just one of the minute living wonders of the world.

Finding out more

Books like this one only give a brief introduction to a subject such as phytoplankton. Some other useful reference books are:

Mary M Cerullo, *Sea Soup Phytoplankton*, Tilbury House Publishers, 1999
Deboyd L Smith, *A Guide: Marine Coastal Plankton and Marine Invertebrate Larvae*, Kendall/Hunt Publishing Company, 1977

You may also find the following web sites useful:

www.ucmp.berkeley.edu/alllife/threedomains.html
A very comprehensive site about life on Earth. Have a look at the section on the Protoctista.

seawifs.gsfc.nasa.gov/SEAWIFS/LIVING_OCEAN
Contains material about phytoplankton produced by NASA's Office of Mission to Planet Earth.

www.lifesci.ucsb.edu/~biolum
A site that introduces bioluminescence in the sea.

www.redtide.whoi.edu/hab
Contains information about red tides and blooms from Woods Hole Oceanographic Institute. For more general information about the ocean, try www.whoi.edu

www.geo.nsf.gov
Contains information about the world's oceans from the National Science Foundation in the United States.

As urls (web site addresses) may change, you may have trouble finding a site listed here. If this happens, you can still use the key words highlighted throughout the book to search for information about a topic.

Glossary

cell: A microscopic structure that is the basic unit of all life. Animals and plants are all multi-celled (made of many cells); fungi are mainly multi-celled; protoctists are almost all single-celled, and bacteria are all single-celled

cellulose: The substance from which wood is made. Dinoflagellates also use cellulose to make protective plates

compound microscope: A microscope with two or more lenses that makes an image of an object larger by passing light through it; this creates a color image

lenses: Pieces of glass (or other transparent substances) that bend light rays. Lenses are often used to create a magnified image of an object

metric system: A system of measurement that uses the meter as its basic unit

microbes: Any microscopic organisms, such as bacteria

multi-celled: Any organism that is made of more than one cell

organisms: Living things

oxygen: A gas that makes up around 21 percent of the Earth's atmosphere. Animals need oxygen to survive

phytoplankton: Plant-like organisms that drift about in water. Diatoms and dinoflagellates are both examples of phytoplankton

plankton: Small animals (zooplankton) and plant-like organisms (phytoplankton) that drift or float about in water

plankton net: A fine-mesh net used to collect plankton

red tides: Sudden blooms of toxic dinoflagellates

scanning electron microscope: Also called a sem, this microscope uses a beam of electrons to make the image of an object larger. Sems produce a black and white image, but artificial colors can be added later if required

single-celled: Any organism that is made of only one cell. Single-celled organisms are all microscopic

Index